To my mother and father and to Ray

CUMBERLAND ROAD

First published in Great Britain in 1988 by
PAVILION BOOKS LIMITED
196 Shaftesbury Avenue, London WC2H 8JL
in association with Michael Joseph Limited
27 Wrights Lane, Kensington, London W8 5TZ

Designed by Tom Sawyer

British Library Cataloguing in Publication Data
Smith, Barry
Can you find? : Cumberland road.
1. Houses – For children
I. Title
643'.6

ISBN 1 85145 231 1

Printed in Belgium by Henri Proost & Cie, Turnhout

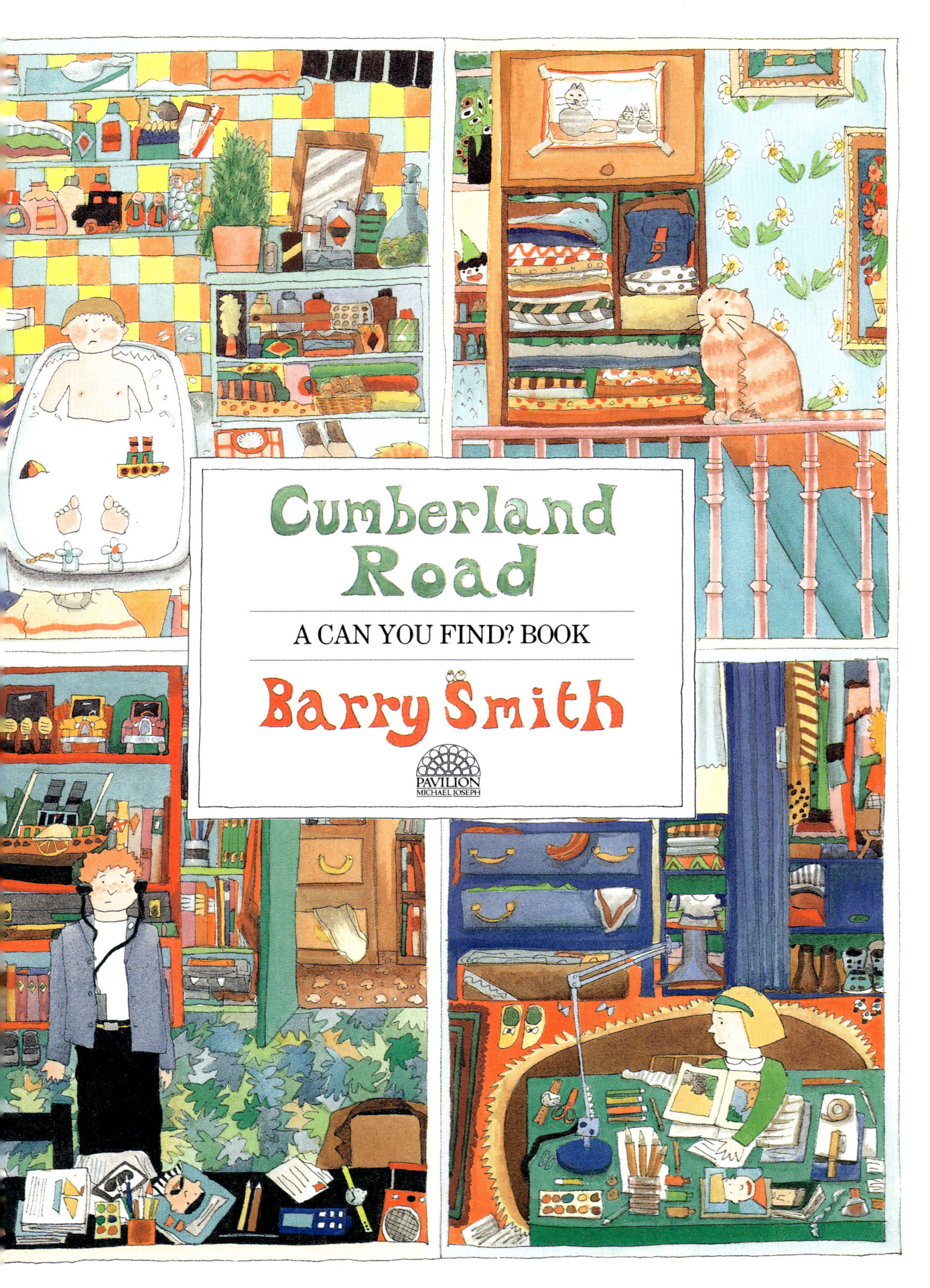

Cumberland Road

A CAN YOU FIND? BOOK

Barry Smith

PAVILION
MICHAEL JOSEPH

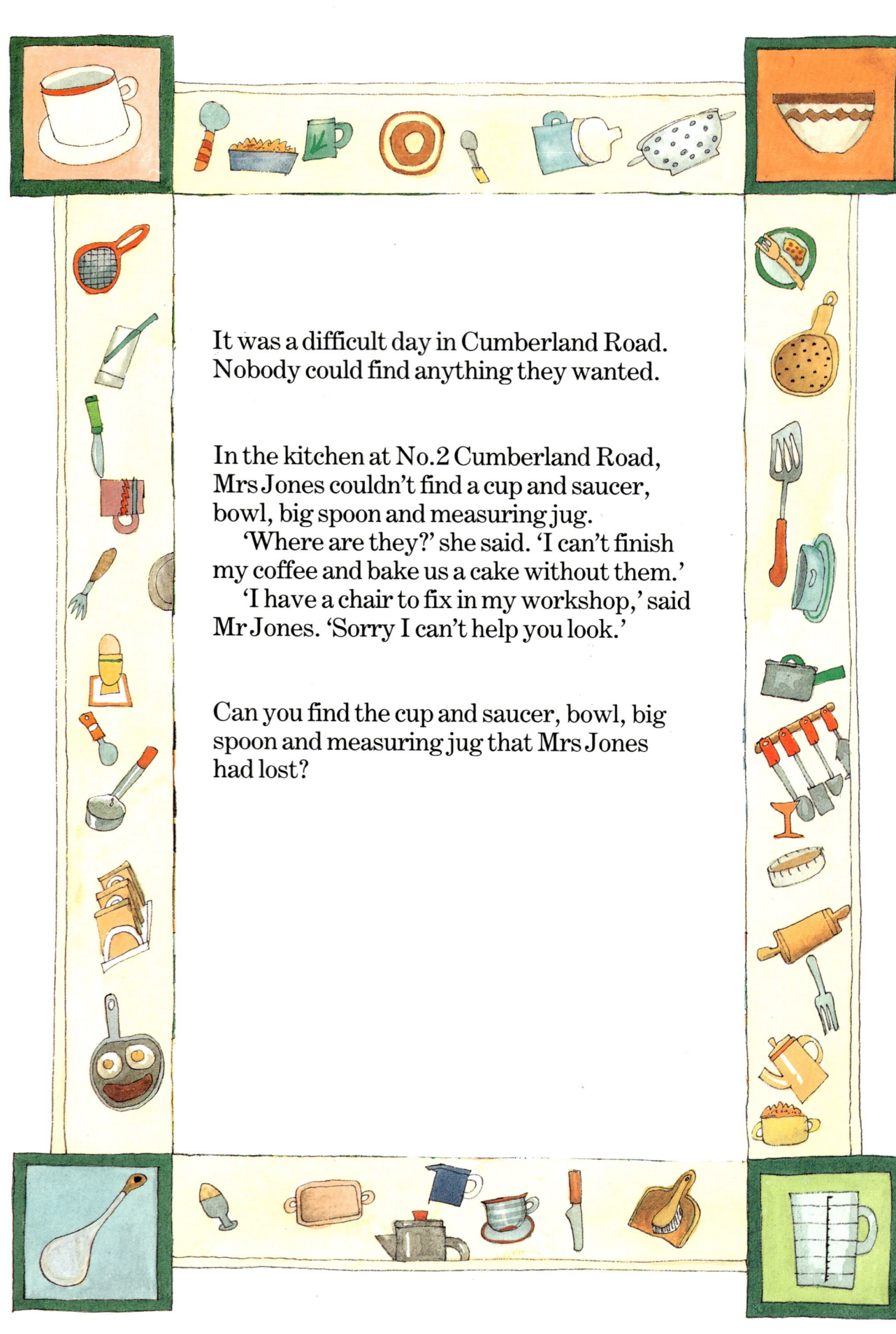

It was a difficult day in Cumberland Road.
Nobody could find anything they wanted.

In the kitchen at No.2 Cumberland Road,
Mrs Jones couldn't find a cup and saucer,
bowl, big spoon and measuring jug.

   'Where are they?' she said. 'I can't finish
my coffee and bake us a cake without them.'

   'I have a chair to fix in my workshop,' said
Mr Jones. 'Sorry I can't help you look.'

Can you find the cup and saucer, bowl, big
spoon and measuring jug that Mrs Jones
had lost?

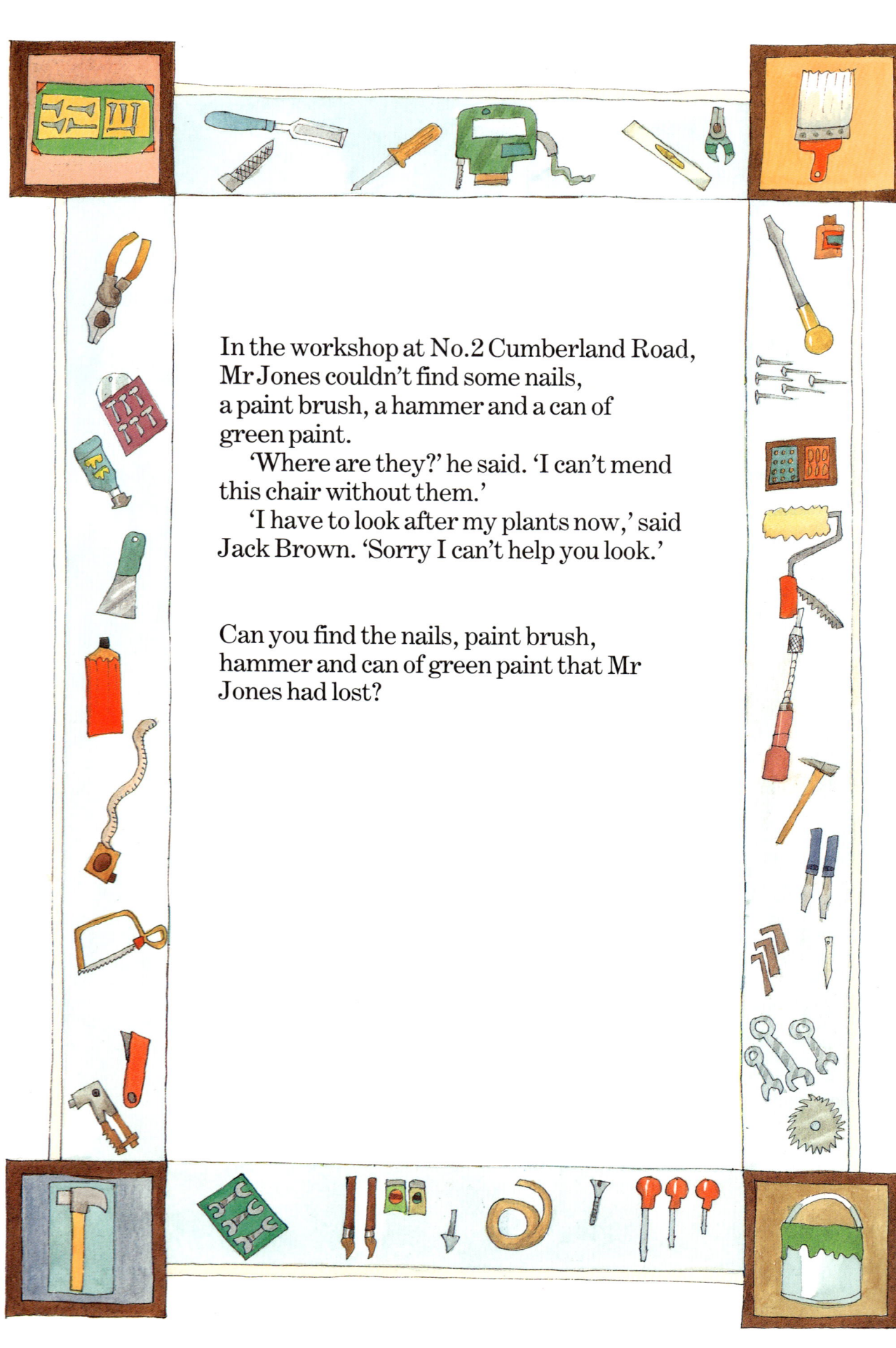

In the workshop at No. 2 Cumberland Road,
Mr Jones couldn't find some nails,
a paint brush, a hammer and a can of
green paint.

'Where are they?' he said. 'I can't mend
this chair without them.'

'I have to look after my plants now,' said
Jack Brown. 'Sorry I can't help you look.'

Can you find the nails, paint brush,
hammer and can of green paint that Mr
Jones had lost?

In the greenhouse at No. 4 Cumberland Road, Jack Brown couldn't find his trowel, watering can, empty pots for plants and gardening gloves.

'Where are they?' he said. 'I can't look after my plants without them.'

'I have to get ready to visit relatives,' said Kevin. 'Sorry I can't help you look.'

Can you find the trowel, watering can, empty pots for plants and gardening gloves that Jack Brown had lost?

In the bathroom at No.6 Cumberland Road, Kevin couldn't find his bath sponge, towel, toy duck and soap.

'Where are they?' he said. 'I can't have my bath without them.'

'I have to mend my dress before we go out,' said Kevin's mother. 'Sorry I can't help you look.'

Can you find the bath sponge, towel, toy duck and soap that Kevin had lost?

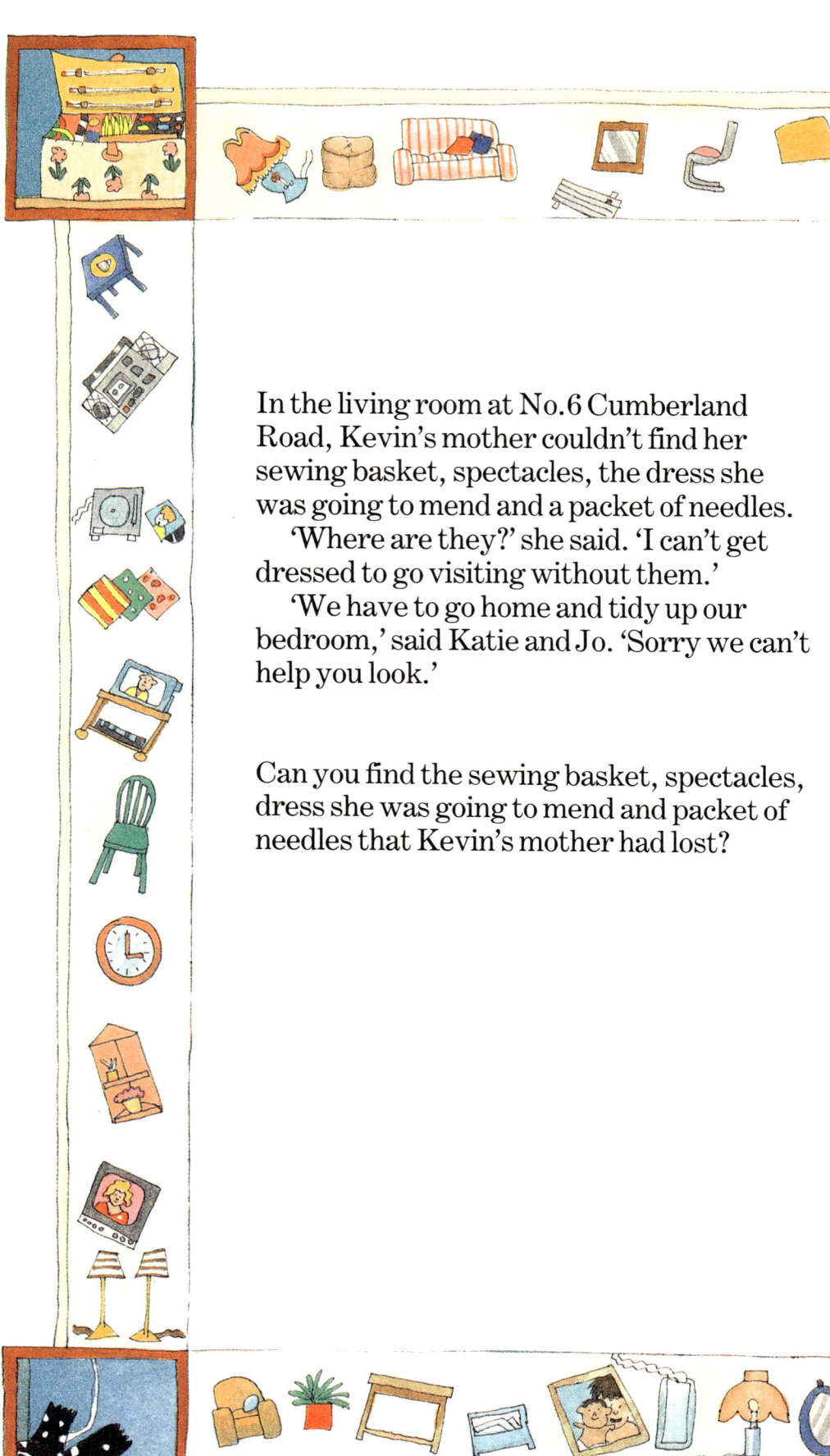

In the living room at No.6 Cumberland Road, Kevin's mother couldn't find her sewing basket, spectacles, the dress she was going to mend and a packet of needles.

'Where are they?' she said. 'I can't get dressed to go visiting without them.'

'We have to go home and tidy up our bedroom,' said Katie and Jo. 'Sorry we can't help you look.'

Can you find the sewing basket, spectacles, dress she was going to mend and packet of needles that Kevin's mother had lost?

In their bedroom on the top floor at No.8 Cumberland Road, Katie and Jo couldn't find their yellow school bags, green shoes, pencil sharpeners shaped like butterflies and their red hair ribbons.

'Where are they?' they said. 'We can't go to school without them.'

'I have to do my homework now,' said Sandra. 'Sorry I can't help you look.'

Can you find the yellow school bags, green shoes, butterfly-shaped pencil sharpeners and red hair ribbons that Katie and Jo had lost?

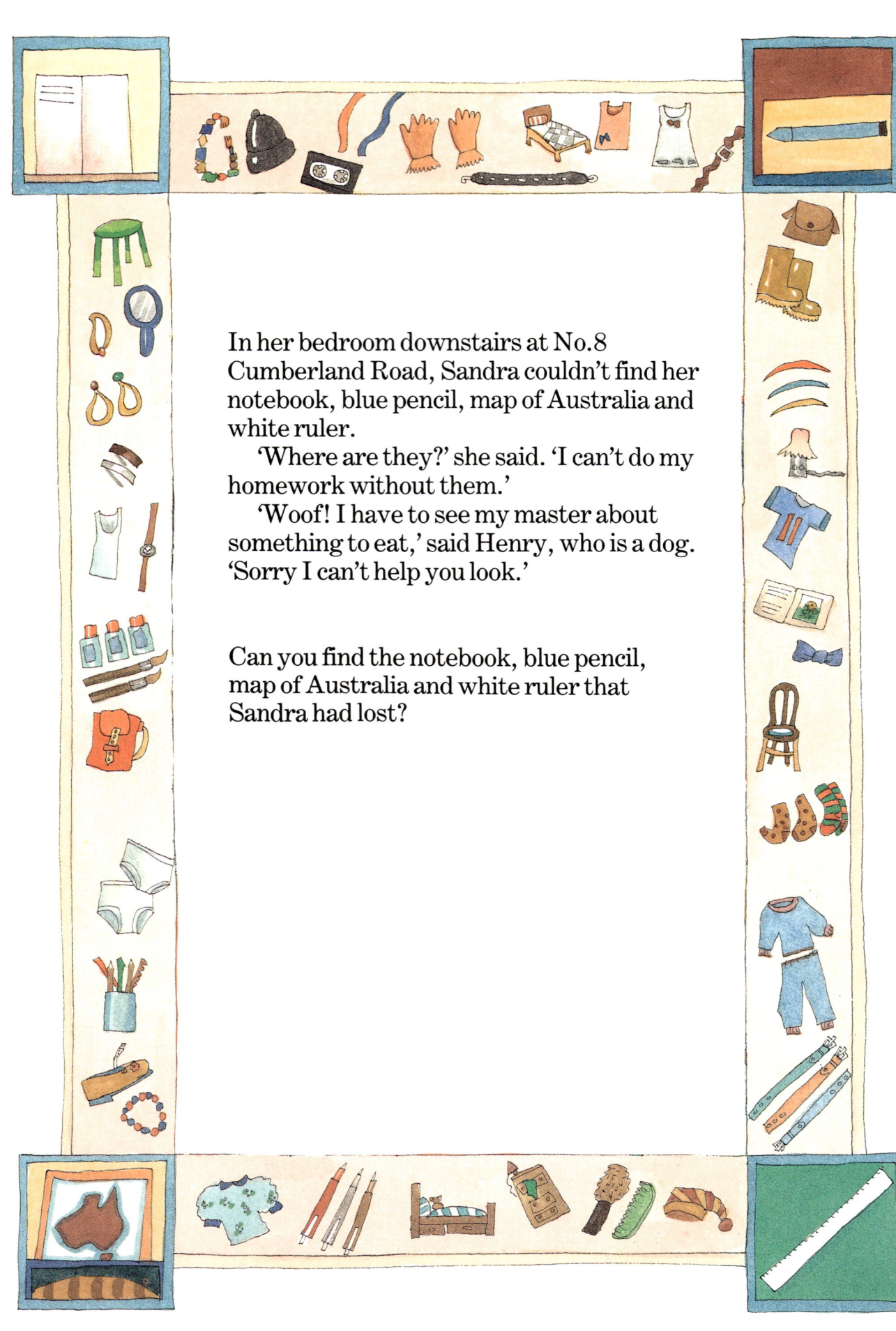

In her bedroom downstairs at No.8 Cumberland Road, Sandra couldn't find her notebook, blue pencil, map of Australia and white ruler.

'Where are they?' she said. 'I can't do my homework without them.'

'Woof! I have to see my master about something to eat,' said Henry, who is a dog. 'Sorry I can't help you look.'

Can you find the notebook, blue pencil, map of Australia and white ruler that Sandra had lost?

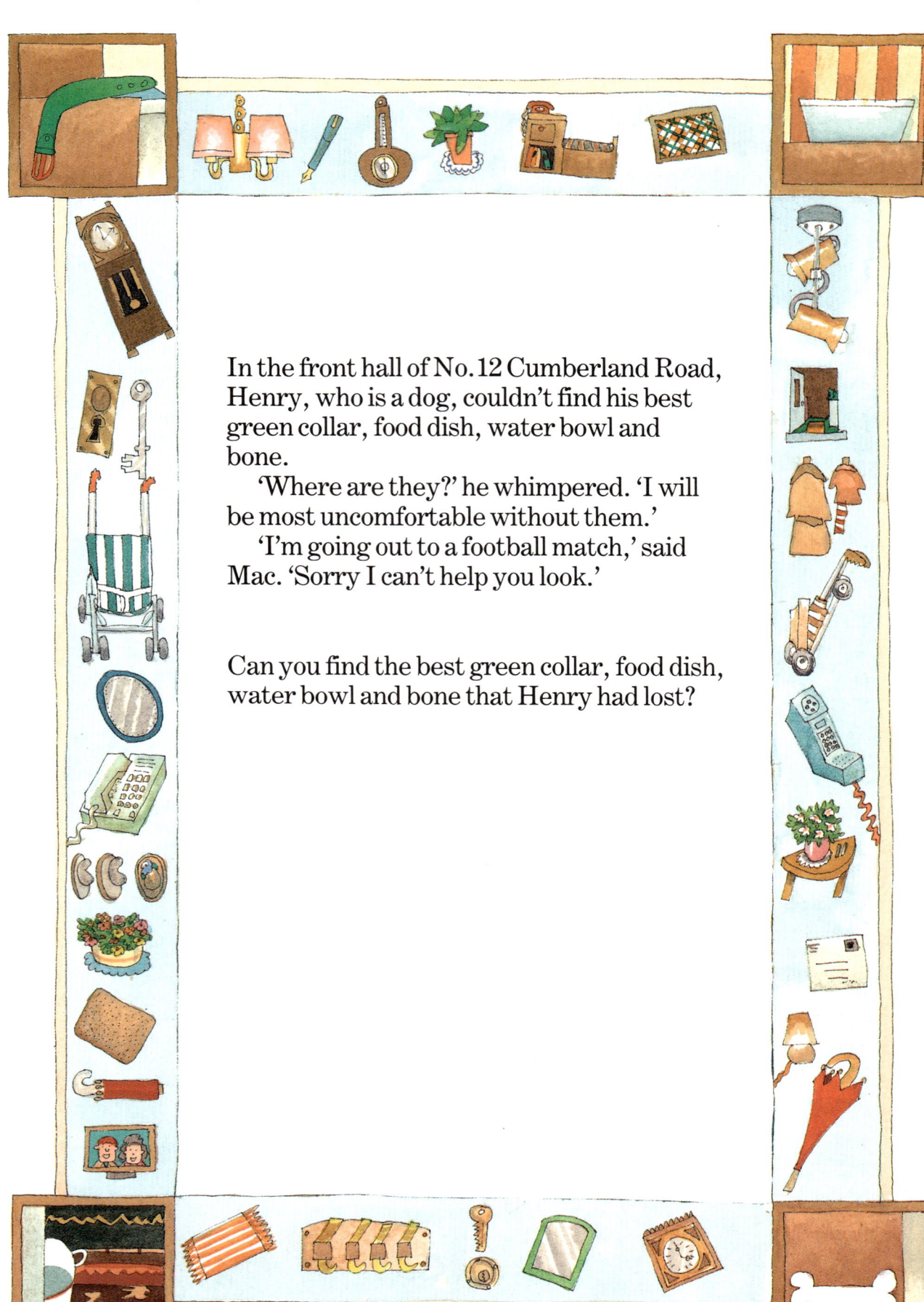

In the front hall of No. 12 Cumberland Road, Henry, who is a dog, couldn't find his best green collar, food dish, water bowl and bone.

'Where are they?' he whimpered. 'I will be most uncomfortable without them.'

'I'm going out to a football match,' said Mac. 'Sorry I can't help you look.'

Can you find the best green collar, food dish, water bowl and bone that Henry had lost?

In his bedroom at No. 12 Cumberland Road, Mac couldn't find his tickets for the match, binoculars, cap and camera.

'Where are they?' he said. 'We won't be able to go without them.'

'I have to check the car before the match,' said Mac's friend Billy. 'Sorry I can't help you look.'

Can you find the tickets for the match, binoculars, cap and camera that Mac had lost?

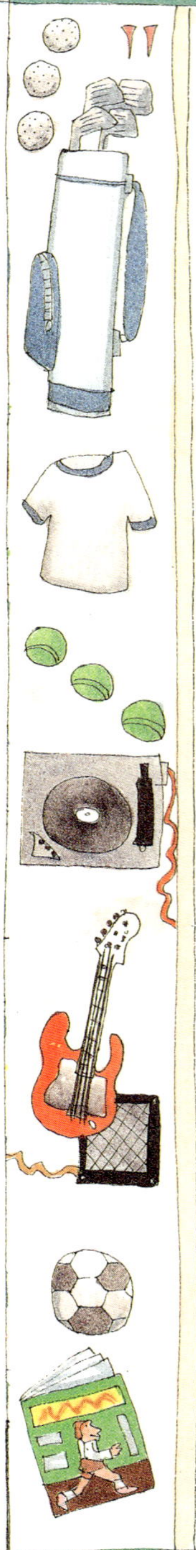

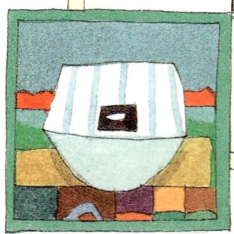

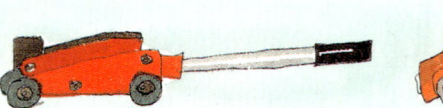

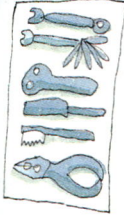

In the garage at No. 10 Cumberland Road,
Mac's friend Billy couldn't find his wallet,
car key, sunglasses and road map.

'Where are they?' he said. 'We'll never
get to the match without them.'

'Now I have to see my dear friend Mr
Goldstone – he's coming to visit,' said Miss
Venetia Grey. 'Sorry I can't help you look.'

Can you find the wallet, car key, sunglasses
and road map that Mac's friend Billy had
lost?

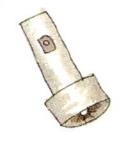

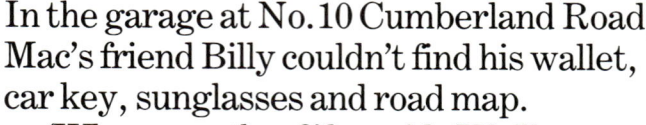

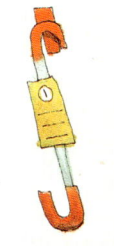

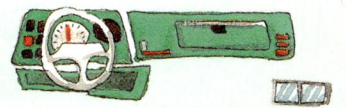

In her parlour at No. 14 Cumberland Road, Miss Venetia Grey couldn't find her warm rug, the novel she was reading, her comfortable slippers and bag of bonbons.

'Where are they?' she said. 'I can't enjoy this evening without them.'

'I have to return Gracie the cat right away,' said Mr Goldstone. 'Sorry I can't help you look.'

Can you find the warm rug, novel she was reading, comfortable slippers and bag of bonbons that Miss Venetia Grey had lost?

In his room at No.4 Cumberland Road, Mr Goldstone couldn't find his teapot, teacup and saucer, milk jug and chocolate cake.

'Where are they?' he said. 'I can't have my supper without them.'

'So what?' miaowed Gracie, who is a fat cat. 'I'm going home. Sorry I can't help you look.'

Can you find the teapot, teacup and saucer, milk jug and chocolate cake that Mr Goldstone had lost?

On the upstairs landing at No.14
Cumberland Road, Gracie the fat cat
couldn't find her red collar, sleeping basket,
rubber mouse and milk dish.

'Where are they?' she miaowed. 'I shan't
sleep at all without them.'

'Oh dear, my baby is crying,' said
Mother. 'Sorry I can't help you look.'

Can you find the red collar, sleeping basket,
rubber mouse and milk dish that Gracie the
fat cat had lost?

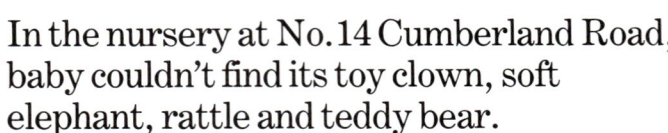

In the nursery at No. 14 Cumberland Road, baby couldn't find its toy clown, soft elephant, rattle and teddy bear.

'Gurgle, gurgle, grizzle and whinge,' said baby.

'Of course I'll help you my dear little baby. I *will* help you look.'

Can you find baby's toy clown, soft elephant, rattle and teddy bear?

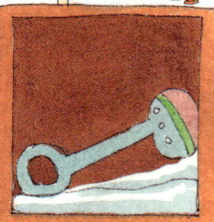

PRINTED IN BELGIUM BY
proost
INTERNATIONAL BOOK PRODUCTION